Fasting for Leaders from the Pulpit to the Pew

Andrea Dardello, Ph.D., CPC

Fasting for Leaders from the Pulpit to the Pew

Twenty-One Days to Find Your Godly Purpose

TATE PUBLISHING
AND ENTERPRISES, LLC

Published by Tate Publishing & Enterprises, LLC
127 E. Trade Center Terrace | Mustang, Oklahoma 73064 USA
1.888.361.9473 | www.tatepublishing.com

Tate Publishing is committed to excellence in the publishing industry. The company reflects the philosophy established by the founders, based on Psalm 68:11,
"The Lord gave the word and great was the company of those who published it."

Cover design by Joel Uber
Interior design by Nathan Harmony

Published in the United States of America

ISBN: 978-1-62024-123-3
1. Religion / Christian Life / Spiritual Growth
2. Religion / Christian Life / Personal Growth
12.06.20

Acknowledgments

I am grateful to all who were a part of this journey. To my mom, Mattie Duckworth, without whom this work would not be possible. Thank you for all of your support and for birthing me so that I could birth this work.

To Rev. Reginald Pickett, thank you for initiating the process by prompting me to write. A special shout-out to those who read and provided feedback for one of the many, many, many drafts of this book: Jennifer Matthews, Natalie Pickett, Elisa Roberson, Lily Ifield, Stacy Richardson, Debbie Barnes, Denise Starrett, and Liz Fisch. Thank you all for helping me to write in a way that readers could receive and understand. A very special thank you goes to my editor, Jessica Browning, who helped bring the full vision of this book into focus.

Thank you, Bruce Schneider—my mentor, coach, and teacher—for taking the time to read my book. Thank you for challenging me to create the reality of my dreams. Your vote of confidence about this work means more to me than you will ever know.

I'd also like to thank my husband, Darryl, who knew there was a book inside of me long before I did. Thank you for being comfortable in your own skin while at the same time pushing me to be more. A special thanks to our little Bakari ("promised one") who inspires me with every smile and breath.

Finally, I give all praises to God, the true inspiration for this book. Your promises are yes and amen. It is so!

Table of Contents

Introduction

At the beginning of 2011, I entered a corporate fast with my church family but started a week early because I was desperate. On the outside, it seemed I had everything—a supportive husband, a thriving two-year old son, a Ph.D., and a full professorship at the college where I teach. Everything on the "to-do" list I created in sixth grade had been marked off, yet my restlessness signaled to me that something was still missing. There was more that I needed to do, and I was determined to find out what it was.

Something happened to me at the age of forty. Like many "forty-somethings," I just wanted to cut to the chase and to start truly living. More frequent reports of friends who had made their transition from this life to the next forced me to think about the quality of my own life and whether or not I was making the impact I truly wanted to make. I looked up and realized that forty years had passed, and I had not yet accomplished all that I wanted. For most of my adult life, I had been waiting for my moment to shine; I had been waiting for my moment to lead—to make the most of the talents God had given me to help others. Somewhere along the way, I had gotten comfortable with being in the background. I admit, it was safest there, out of the reach of scrutiny, criticism, and potential conflict.

But while it was safe, the background also left me wandering aimlessly. This lack of direction made me restless. I knew I had too much to give, and I became more determined than ever to give it. However, I wasn't sure of what I was supposed to be doing or how to go about doing it. I was determined not to waste another minute of my life. God was calling me to do something greater and now that He had gotten my attention, I needed to be clear of the direction I would take. So when the pastor called for a fast, I was the first to sign up. But because I was seeking real answers, this fast would be different. I didn't just want to go through the motions. I wanted to understand what fasting was, and most importantly, I wanted results! At the end of the fast, I wanted to feel confident that I was being led by God.

So, unlike other times when I had fasted, I actually developed a plan for my fast. Two weeks prior, I had read Jentezen Franklin's book *Fasting*[1] and got vegan recipes from Susan Gregory's book, *The Daniel Fast.*[2] I followed Franklin's prayer guide in his *Fasting Journal*[3] and found scriptures to accompany each day's topic. I kept an extensive journal, recording changes that were happening both inside me and around me.

Some changes I consciously made, and others were solely divine. These changes, the ones of which I had no control, I counted as miracles. I experienced more miraculous moments as I learned truly to let go and trust God completely with my life—even the details I had not yet worked out. I also downloaded songs to my iPod that spoke to my specific needs at the time.

The more I prepared for the fast, the more excited I became. Unlike other times, I was not fasting simply because everyone else was doing it. This time, I fasted to know more about God and what He wanted from me. Not only did I expect an answer, I expected something great. Each day, I looked for a miracle, and each day, I received one whether it was a new insight about how I desired to live my life, a revelation about where I truly was in my walk with God, or direct and specific answers to requests I had made of God.

On the second day of my fast, God answered the big question about what it is that I was supposed to be doing, and you are reading it now. He led me to write a book about how to help others fast successfully using the skills I had developed as a life coach. I had been struggling with the decision either to follow my passion or to do what was expected of me. In the academic community, those who hold doctoral degrees are warned to "publish or perish." I realized that the reason I had not published was because I was trying to fulfill someone else's dream rather my own. The expectations of others in my field that I should gain recognition and prominence by writing for academic journals did not fit in with what I truly wanted for my life. Fasting freed me to pursue my two passions: the Bible and coaching. This clarity of direction has made me happier and more content than I have ever been, so it is my joy to share with you what I have learned.

Why Fast?

A 2010 study by the Pew Forum on Religious Life indicated that 25 percent of young people between the ages of 18 and 29 are less likely to attend church or claim any religious affiliation than the generation that came before it. That's 5 percent more than the previous generation (those of us who were that age in the 90s) and nearly double that number (13 percent) for Baby Boomers who came of age in the seventies.[4] These statistics bear witness to the major claim of Jentezen Franklin's latest book, *The Fasting Edge,* that the church is losing its edge or its ability to effectively minister and change lives. Franklin declares, "I am tired of services where we just go through the motions and leave just as we came."[5] I am a witness and couldn't agree more. Like the churchgoers Franklin references here, I also spent years in the church only to find myself burdened with many of the same issues I had when I first joined. While I enjoyed worship services in the moment, I lacked the knowledge of how to take the message I heard on Sunday and use it to transform my life. Franklin attributes this unproductive cycle to the lack of focus given to individual and corporate fasting.

While some churches omit fasting altogether because of their claim that it is not a Biblical requirement,[6] others initiate fasts without any planning, focus, or direction. Given the present state of our society and our world, this lack of attention to fasting is always surprising to me, since it is the way we access God's power to do the extraordinary. While Jesus's disciples failed to heal the child who constantly fell into fire and water, Jesus could. The disciples asked why they were not able to heal him, and Jesus's reply was "…this kind goeth not out but by prayer and fasting" (Matthew 17:17, KJV). This scripture makes it clear that if we want to see greater results in our lives, if we want to do more than the ordinary, we must fast *and* pray. Stovall Weems aptly writes that "[God] is a filler, not a forcer"[7] so for those who choose not to fast, it is their option, but because I know firsthand the deliverance that can come through fasting, I am compelled to run and tell others about it.

Spiritual fasting is often defined as the willful act of going without food for a period of time for a spiritual purpose. In *Celebration of the Disciplines,* Richard Foster emphatically states that "Biblical fasting *always* centers on spiritual purposes" [italics added].[8] However, the problem with many individual and corporate fasts is that only the first part of the definition is taken into consideration when the fast is called. Any spiritual fast that only focuses on abstaining from food without any attention to the purpose for which the fast is called is merely a fast for dieting or health reasons. While these types of fasts certainly have their place, fasting without a purpose for the spiritual community means limiting the growth and the power of those who are a part of it.

I write not as an expert on fasting, per se, but rather as a lifelong member of the Church who has been summoned to fast on numerous occasions, not fully understanding what it was that I was supposed to be doing (beyond going without food) or what I was supposed to have taken from the experience (beyond feeling really proud of myself). It wasn't until

I developed a deep longing in my heart to carry out God's purpose for my life that I began to study what God had to say about the type of fast that was pleasing unto Him and truly began to experience the joy and fulfillment that are a result of *purposeful* fasting. I emphasize the word purpose here because that is the essence of all God-appointed fasts. We fast to discover how God can best use us for His purpose. I was in my forties when this epiphany occurred, and I could not help but think of how much time I had lost by not grasping the power of prayer and fasting—power that was always available to me ever since I invited God into my heart at the age of ten. If I can help someone accelerate the rate at which they realize their dreams and do more with their lives even at half my age, I will have accomplished the goal of this book. This is my prayer even as I am writing to you now.

In *Fasting for Spiritual Breakthrough,* Elmer Towns outlines at least nine issues the Scriptures address through fasting.[9] Each issue is connected to a desired purpose or outcome. They are: 1) the Disciple's Fast, for deliverance from addictions and other strongholds, 2) The Daniel Fast, for health, 3) the John the Baptist Fast, for the power to influence others for Christ, 4) the Esther Fast, for protection, 5) the St. Paul Fast, for decision-making, 6) the Widow's Fast, to bring awareness of hunger and suffering throughout the world, 7) the Elijah Fast, for leaders of integrity and strength, 8) the Ezra Fast, for finding solutions to problems, and 9) the Samuel Fast, for re-energizing God's people to carry out His work. Towns is clear that while these fasts are not all-inclusive, the fast or fasts that are chosen should accomplish a purpose in the believer's life.[10] When we fast to gain insights about how to live our lives more effectively, we begin to fast with purpose.

By default, many Churches defer to the Daniel Fast, I imagine only because of its recent popularity from books like Jentezen Franklin's *Fasting*. But with 27.1 million Americans suffering from heart disease[11] and another 19.4 million having been diagnosed with cancer in 2010 alone,[12] it is appropriate that this particular fast which focuses on health is also accompanied by discussions of proper diet, screenings and information sessions about diseases that plague our age, including obesity, cancer, heart disease, AIDS and HIV. These are the types of activities that bring home the purpose of the Daniel Fast and address the issues upon which this particular fast is based.

But because the whole of our spiritual needs extends beyond health, the other fasts that Towns references are worth considering as well. For example, during this time of economic recession, joblessness, and foreclosures, there should also be calls for the Disciple's Fast, where along with giving up trips to shopping malls and simplifying our lives, fasting participants are educated about how to manage and save money in ways that enable them to meet the future without fear. This is the type of fast relevant to the modern age and that is carried out strategically, with a specific purpose in mind. The holistic approach to fasting that I am advocating here not only creates a buy-in for the fast, but makes the goal of the fast tangible. A purposeful fast seeks desired results, such as healthier lifestyles, balanced budgets, clearer financial planning and an overall heightened sense of awareness and freedom.

The results that I am speaking about are not those that simply please the self, but benefit the body of Christ and ministers to others. The evidence of spiritual fasting is important since it provides the testimony for both the effectiveness of fasting as well as for the church and its ministries. Imagine members leaving your church and going to tell their friends not merely that they had a "good" time in service but through prayer and fasting were delivered from strongholds that held them captive for years. What would that testimony mean for your ministry once you start honing in on the needs of those you serve?

Imagine being freed up financially from paying members' electric bills because you will, through purposeful fasting, have also taught them how to manage their budgets. Imagine these same members being freed from harassing phone calls and living in fear of eviction notices because through goal-centered, action-oriented fasting, you've helped them to help themselves. Now, imagine those same people, now knowing how to better manage their finances, having monies to pour into your ministry. They do so out a willing spirit because, like Jesus did on so many occasions, you satisfied a deeper longing, one that couldn't be satisfied solely by weekly doses of song, scripture, and sermons. Rather, you upped the ante because you realized the power that comes forth through prayer and fasting.

If you are still wondering if fasting is for you, your ministry, or church, then consider some of the benefits that have been associated with food fasts, including healing our bodies by fighting infection,[13] ridding our bodies of wastes and poisons,[14] slowing down aging,[15] reducing the risks of heart attack,[16] and increasing concentration.[17] While these benefits are significant, it is equally important to note here that those engaging in food fasts should consult their physicians first.

Dr. Rex Russell goes on to point out mental benefits, such as reducing stress, improving our ability to reason, creating a feeling of overall balance, and preventing addictions to food.[18] Now, this is not to suggest that fasting should replace medical intervention when it is required. Lynne Baab warns that "When a habit involves a life-damaging addiction, we need to take serious action such as medical treatment or participation in Alcoholics Anonymous or other support groups. The central purpose of Christian fasting is to clear away daily pleasures so we can approach God in new ways. Fasting is not medical treatment or a temporary cure for sinfulness."[19]

And certainly there are spiritual benefits, which include a heightened awareness of God's presence in our lives as well as a greater awareness of our tendencies to place our excesses before God.[20] Other spiritual benefits include interceding on behalf of others more effectively, guidance in decision-making, and receiving insights from God.[21] In both *Fasting* and *The Fasting Edge,* Jentezen Franklin has strongly argued that fasting is a way to accelerate God's plan for our lives. Indeed, when we choose to participate in a God-appointed fast, when the purpose of the fast is clear, and when the vision for the fast is made plain, everyone benefits.

What Is This Book and Who Is It For?

With the previous chapter's focus on purposeful fasting, I hear some of you asking, "But what if you are new to the faith and are uncertain about God's voice? What role, then, does fasting play in the life of the New Christian? How, if you're not used to God's voice, do you hear Him to access that purpose? What happens if you feel a strong tugging in your chest, leading you to do *something*, but you don't yet know what it is?" Hold on. I haven't forgotten about you. Keep reading.

In the first book of Kings, the nineteenth chapter, the prophet Elijah goes into a cave to fast for forty days and forty nights to seek direction from God. While he is waiting, a strong wind comes, followed by an earthquake and then a fire. The scriptures tell us that God was in neither of these, but rather, He came in a "still, small voice." This book was written to acquaint or reacquaint people with that "still, small voice" that continues to live in each of us. If we dare to listen to it, we, like Elijah, will gain clarity of direction for our lives. However, many times we fail to hear God because we are distracted by the noise and commotion that surrounds us. Therefore, this book is designed to be used when you are undisturbed and still enough to hear that small voice inside of you. This could be any time you choose—perhaps during a period of fasting or perhaps during some other time you have designated for quiet reflection and meditation. Whenever you choose to use this book, know that it was written to help you hear from God so that you know without question the work He has called you to do.

The word "work" is important because this book is written for those willing and ready to do the inner work necessary to be effective leaders of self, family, and community. This work is intimately tied to God's purpose for each of us to lead ourselves and others to be better. The conscious choice to carry out God's purpose requires reflecting on God's Word and being able to thoughtfully apply it to our lives. The truth of the matter is that sometimes we don't know what scriptures address our situation, and if we do, we haven't taken the time to truly think about them.

I have responded to this need by providing scriptures that address the major issues surrounding leadership and by providing space to write down what God is saying to you through His word. God commands the prophet in Habakkuk 2:2 to "[w]rite the vision, and make it plain…that he [and she] may run that readeth it" (KJV). The act of writing, then, not only allows us to physically see what God has revealed to us inwardly, but writing also provides a permanent record to remind us of what God said He would do through us. The ability to refer to this promise can motivate us to start and finish the race set before us to run. In short, then, this book is written to get you moving on what God wants you to do.

Because from the womb each and every one of us was designed with a specific purpose in mind (see Isaiah 49), this book is for anyone. It is also important to note that as we grow and change, so does our purpose. This book, then, is also ideal for anyone experiencing or thinking about changing something in their lives, but haven't because of fear, uncertainty, or because of lack of support from family and friends.

This book is equally important for anyone looking to serve others in any form, including but not limited to, preaching, teaching, singing, or working with youth, adults, singles, or married couples. It is for those who know what they have been called to do but do not yet know how to go about it. It is for those already in positions of leadership who desire to lead more effectively. It is for those who realize that the major task of leading first begins with "self" and so wish to examine their own lives more closely. In short, this book is for anyone seeking to lead a more meaningful life.

How This Book Is Organized

The remaining chapters in this book are devoted to helping you identify and carry out your purpose through fasting. "Fasting with New Focus" takes readers through a close reading of Isaiah 58, which points out common misinterpretations of fasting and brings to light the ultimate reason God desires us to fast.

"Rethinking Fasting to Get to Your Purpose" elaborates on how fasting can help us better lead ourselves and others. Several examples from the Bible are given to demonstrate why those in leadership ought to fast and to clarify further the type of fast that is pleasing unto God.

"Strategies for a Successful Fast" walks you through two exercises that help you establish your own personal reason for fasting. This chapter also introduces you to the SMARTT-FAST system that is designed to help you plan a successful fast.

"Recognizing, Preparing, and Developing the Leader in You" is the spiritual work-out part of the book. Designed to be used over a twenty-one day period, this chapter addresses three phases of leadership:

1. Knowing yourself, your God, and your purpose
2. Doing the inner work that prepares you to lead effectively
3. Preparing to lead others

A specific topic is selected for each day and is accompanied with motivational songs, scriptures, and prayers. Journal activities encourage you to reflect on God's Word and to act on what that word reveals to you.

"Coming Off of Your Fast" provides tips and strategies for celebrating the culmination of your fast and continuing the work revealed to you during your fasting season.

Finally, in "Leading Others to Fast Successfully," I provide specific strategies for elevating corporate fasts beyond ritual to one that produces life-changing results.

To summarize, the following awaits you in this book:

- an explanation of what fasting is and how it is connected to your purpose
- exercises that help you realize your own purpose for fasting and help you get excited about what is possible for your life
- the SMARTT-FAST system that helps you develop a plan to succeed with your fast
- a twenty-one day meditative guide for your fast, complete with motivational songs, scriptures, journal activities and pro-active prayers

- self-directed and self-paced action steps that move you closer to becoming the leader God has called you to be
- specific strategies for leading corporate or group fasts

Fasting with New Focus

In preparation for fasting, I studied many scriptures, but it was Isaiah 58 that opened my eyes to the type of fast that truly pleases God and helped me to realize why my fasts had not been successful in the past. This scripture, like none other, would take my experience with fasting to a completely different level. It took me beyond just going through the motions of fasting and helped me to understand what it meant to fast with a purpose and why such a fast is pleasing to God. It is the only scripture that devotes an entire chapter to the subject of fasting. The directives about fasting are from God, spoken by the prophet. With this realization, I've made Isaiah 58 the anchor for this book, and for this reason, I have included it in its entirety. Every idea and exercise contained in this book is based on a new understanding of fasting as revealed in Isaiah 58.

The text opens with God angry and disappointed in a people so busy with the ritual of fasting that they could no longer hear Him:

> Shout! A full-throated shout! Hold nothing back—a trumpet-blast shout! Tell my people what's wrong with their lives, face my family Jacob with their sins! They're busy, busy, busy at worship, and love studying all about me. To all appearances they're a nation of right-living people—law-abiding, God-honoring. They ask me, 'What's the right thing to do?' and love having me on their side. But they also complain, 'Why do we fast and you don't look our way? Why do we humble ourselves and you don't even notice?'
>
> Isaiah 58:1-2 (The Message)

I had several "aha" moments as I began to see myself in these people with whom God had become greatly displeased. Here was a well-meaning people so engaged with the act of fasting that they had forgotten about the reason they were fasting—to connect to their God and to draw closer to Him. Immediately, I began to think about the times I had fasted in the past and how the Lenten season would come, and because it was just what Christians were expected to do, I would give up chocolate or meat or some other thing that I truly loved because I thought the act of giving up what I physically desired would be pleasing to God. But what Isaiah 58 was telling me was that giving up food alone was not enough to get God's attention. In fact, it was the obsession with the ritualistic aspects of fasting that caused God to look away.

I realized that God had stopped paying attention because the Israelites had made the act of giving up food more about them and less about Him. They were more concerned with how fasting made them look in the eyes of each other. They had become the focus of their fast—not God. I was like the Israelites who identified fasting with the act of appearing "good" or "holy." As we all know, keeping up appearances can be exhausting. It was no wonder then that fasting became something that I would get through rather than be excited about. There really was no point to my fast, and like the Israelites, I had missed the opportunity to connect with God.

The irony of these verses also struck me. These people were so caught up in the ritual that they became too busy for the God to whom they were fasting. But much more than the sacrifice of food, God desired the Israelites' time. This caused me to think about my own fasting relationship and to be truthful, giving up chocolate was easy since I had every intention of returning to it in twenty-one days, or in the case of Lent, forty days. Giving up my time would mean getting up earlier. It would mean being still, seeking, listening, and even changing. This type of fast would move me from *doing* or *acting* holy to *being* holy—a much more deliberate and powerful choice.

Because I was able to identify with the Israelites in this passage, I saw my fasting relationship with God more clearly. I recognized my neglect and wanted to take responsibility for my actions or lack thereof. I would start by further listening to why the Israelites' fast became meaningless to God, so I read on:

> Well, here's why: The bottom line on your 'fast days' is profit. You drive your employees much too hard. You fast, but at the same time you bicker and fight. You fast, but you swing a mean fist. The kind of fasting you do won't get your prayers off the ground. Do you think this is the kind of fast day

> I'm after: a day to show off humility? To put on a pious long face and parade around solemnly in black? Do you call that fasting, a fast day that I, God, would like?
>
> Isaiah 58:3-5 (The Message)

Verse three registered with me deeply. While I realized this verse was aimed at employers who had taken advantage of the fasting season to drive their workers harder for profit, I began to make connections between the relationship the heartless employers had with their employees and my fasting relationship with God. I truly became remorseful for all the times I had fasted for profit, thinking only of how fasting could benefit me. I considered how ridiculous it was for me to expect God to do something earth-shattering because I had temporarily given up chocolate. Just as the unscrupulous employee overworked his employer for little pay, I had high expectations of God but had given Him little in return. Just as the untrustworthy employee had taken advantage of his employee, I had taken advantage of my fasting relationship with God. Like the Israelites, I had treated God as if He were a servant to my own desires. It was the utter sign of disrespect. No wonder God was so angry, and it was no wonder that after years of fasting I was still unfulfilled. Like the Israelites, I meant well, but I really had no clue about how to please God during my fast. Verses six through fourteen helped me to get clear:

> This is the kind of fast day I'm after: to break the chains of injustice, get rid of exploitation in the workplace, free the oppressed, cancel debts. What I'm interested in seeing you do is: sharing your food with the hungry, inviting the homeless poor into your homes, putting clothes on the shivering ill-clad, being available to your own families. Do this and the lights will turn on, and your lives will turn around at once. Your righteousness will pave your way. The God of glory will secure your passage. Then when you pray, God will answer. You'll call out for help and I'll say, 'Here I am.' If you get rid of unfair practices, quit blaming victims, quit gossiping about other people's sins, If you are generous with the hungry and start giving yourselves to the down-and-out, Your lives will begin to glow in the darkness, your shadowed lives will be bathed in sunlight. I will always show you

> where to go. I'll give you a full life in the emptiest of places—firm muscles, strong bones. You'll be like a well-watered garden, a gurgling spring that never runs dry. You'll use the old rubble of past lives to build anew, rebuild the foundations from out of your past. You'll be known as those who can fix anything, restore old ruins, rebuild and renovate, make the community livable again. If you watch your step on the Sabbath and don't use my holy day for personal advantage, If you treat the Sabbath as a day of joy, God's holy day as a celebration, If you honor it by refusing 'business as usual,' making money, running here and there—Then you'll be free to enjoy God! Oh, I'll make you ride high and soar above it all. I'll make you feast on the inheritance of your ancestor Jacob." Yes! God says so!
>
> Isaiah 58:6-14 (The Message)

These verses helped me understand that the type of fasting God desires is the kind that would change me from the inside out, the kind that would create in me compassion that would inspire me to act, and the kind that would empower me to change my situation and to help those around me. These verses provided me the ultimate reality-check; fasting was not just about me! For the very first time, I became crystal-clear about what God wanted from my fast. More than anything, He wanted me to *do* something, and that something was to carry out His purpose of leading myself, my family, and my community to be better.

I understood this process of leading would last a lifetime—not just the designated time I allotted for my fast. Justice would still need to be sought, oppression and suffering would still need to be addressed, the hungry would still need to be fed, the homeless would still need shelter, and I would still need to be available to my family long after my fast was complete. For the first time, I understood that fasting was a way of preparing me for this greater, continuous work that would last a lifetime and extend unto generations. Upon this revelation, I understood that fasting was God's way of preparing me to carry out His purpose for my life. For the first time ever, I had a reason to fast, and it was profound. Giving up chocolate could not even begin to compare to what God wanted from my fast. He didn't want chocolate. He wanted *me*!

In fact, what God wanted me to give up had less to do with what I was putting into my mouth and more to do with what I was allowing in my heart. Verses three through nine revealed those things that God wanted me to release:

- selfishness
- greed
- phoniness
- favoritism/ treating others unfairly
- taking advantage of others
- arguing
- fighting
- dishonesty
- causing harm to others
- debt
- blame
- gossip

It became clear that fasting had a purpose that went far beyond abstaining from certain foods. In fact, in verse seven, God instructs that we use food during our fast to share with those who are less fortunate. Fasting was designed to help us clear out *anything* that gets in the way of improving our lives and the lives of others. I realized I needed to release a lot that day—*fear* being one of those things. But I also realized that releasing sweets, fatty foods, and foods with preservatives could benefit me, as well, so I let them go. Sleeping in? Released it. Watching certain TV shows? Released them. The moment I chose to consciously release what was holding me back from being my best was the moment that fasting went beyond tradition or ritual. No longer did I view it as a burden, but I viewed it as a gift that would help me improve the quality of my life in every way imaginable. At the deepest part of me, this is what I truly wanted.

These latter verses revealed to me that fasting wasn't about my losing; it was about God wanting to give me more, but in order to receive what He had for me, I had to make room for what He had in store because what He wanted to give surpassed what He was asking me to release. Verses eight through fourteen reveal what God wants to give to those who truly fast unto Him:

- enlightenment
- immediate change in your circumstance
- security
- answers to your questions
- help in the time of trouble
- clarity of direction
- contentment
- fulfillment
- abundance
- restoration of what you have lost
- the ability to fix what is broken
- the ability to rebuild what is torn down
- the ability to get through tough situations
- a good reputation

- vitality
- health
- freedom
- invincibility

One of the greatest gifts I received during my fast was true enlightenment (see verse eight). When I set aside time for God during my fast and when I started truly listening to Him, the "lights turned on" for me. I became more aware of what was going on both inside me and around me. Here's an example. Years ago, a friend gave me a famous painting of a group of people processing to a burial. I hung it in my office because it matched the décor. One day during my fast, I saw the painting for the very first time—I mean really *saw* it.

While at one time I appreciated the artistry of the work—the contrasting light and dark hues—that day, it would have to go. It did not matter to me what the artist intended—at that moment, it screamed of death and dying things, and I wanted it out! Only living things had a place in my house. Death, in any form, was no longer welcomed. Once it became clear to me what the painting represented for me, I immediately called out for my husband to remove it. He was so startled by my cry that he ran down the steps to see what the matter was. I simply pointed and asked him to take it down. He laughed as he reached for the painting. Shaking his head, he said half-jokingly, "What took you so long? I've wanted that thing out of here for years."

While some will focus on only the material rewards of fasting, no value can be placed on the peace and fulfillment one receives when walking confidently in God's will. Since the time of my fast, I have rested on God's promise to "secure [my] passage" (verse eight), and He has not disappointed. Even after I completed my fast, I continued the practice of meeting Him every morning at the same time and in the same place. I no longer worry or have fears about my future. I rest solely on Him. This confidence has led me to do what I had only imagined for my life before I truly fasted unto God. This book is but one example.

By the time I got to the end of Isaiah, my spirit jumped for joy. I began to dance before the Lord. Everything that He wanted for me was what I wanted for myself. There was no longer any reason for me to be reluctant about giving up anything during my fast because I had so much more to gain. Because I wanted to capture and relive the energy of that moment, I immediately started thinking of ways I could make my fast enjoyable. I know it sounds like a contradiction. Very few people associate fasting with enjoyment, but verse five of the text suggests that fasting need not be a sad occasion either:

"Do you think this is the kind of fast day I'm after: a day to show off humility? To put on a pious long face and parade around solemnly in black? Do you call that fasting, a fast day that I, God, would like?" (Isaiah 58:5, The Message).

That was it. I declared a *fun* fast. The first thing I did was put God to the test. I kept a record of every new insight, answer to a specific request I had made of God, and miracle. At the end of the day, I would literally count my blessings. This written record provided the evidence that God was indeed working in my life and that the promises made in Isaiah were real.

I also enjoy music, so I downloaded songs to my iPod to encourage me during the fast. I made a CD of these songs and played them while driving to and from work. Because they were songs I had specifically chosen, they were able to fill me where I hungered most. Since I enjoy cooking, I saw the Daniel Fast as a challenge to prepare meals consisting of mainly fruits, vegetables, beans, peas, and whole grains, as Susan Gregory directs in *The Daniel Fast.* [22] I collected recipes and shared them with friends. Because I was involved in a corporate fast, I took joy in the fact that I did not have to fast alone. Some church members and I formed a group on Facebook. We held weekly conference calls that gave us the opportunity to pray for each other, report on our progress, talk about challenges, and share new insights about God and ourselves. Some of these connections have turned into close friendships. By rethinking fasting, I realized that fasting could be fun, and for the first time, I actually looked forward to it.

Isaiah 58 allowed me to think about fasting in ways I never had before. The chart below compares how I thought about fasting in the past with what the Bible reveals to be the type of fast that pleases God. Perhaps you have had many of the same thoughts. Perhaps you, too, have fasted with little to nothing to show for it. If this is the case, I would like to show you step-by-step how you can experience fasting in a way that is not only personally meaningful but that also brings you closer to knowing and carrying out God's plan for your life. The next chapter continues to explore fasting from a new lens. While this chapter has focused on my personal transformation, the next chapter takes you through the first important step to experiencing fasting in a spiritually relevant way: changing your mind-set.

OLD IDEAS **Fasting is...**	**NEW IDEAS** **(based on Isaiah 58)** **Fasting is...**
losing or giving up something.	making room for as well as receiving the best God has in store for me.
a way to score points with God.	a way to draw closer to God to know him intimately.

not eating certain foods.	about releasing thoughts and habits that keep me from offering my best to God and others.
follows ritual and tradition.	leading myself and others in divinely inspired ways.
must be serious and sad.	can be fun and exciting.
about serving my own interests.	about serving God and others.
about giving up something for a period of time.	about fulfilling my purpose over a lifetime.

Rethinking Fasting to Get to Your Purpose

"Don't copy the behavior and customs of this world, but let God transform you into a new person by changing the way you think. Then you will learn to know God's will for you, which is good and pleasing and perfect" (Romans 12:2, NLT).

This book is about experiencing life-changing results through fasting. Regardless of the type of fast you choose, know that fasting is ultimately about emptying yourself of unproductive thoughts, behaviors, and habits to make room for new thoughts, behaviors, and habits that carry you into the places God has promised. When you decide to truly fast unto God, you will begin to understand what you are meant to do and to get clarity on how to go about living your life in ways that truly fulfill you. When you give yourself permission to rethink fasting, you open yourself to being used for God's purpose. Once your desires align with His will, you open yourself to having the life you truly want!

Rethinking the Language of Fasting

Oftentimes when we talk about fasting, we speak about it from the standpoint of loss. One of the basic principles of coaching is that our language reflects our core beliefs, and those beliefs are then translated into feelings that lead to actions. In other words, we create what we ultimately think and feel. This same principle is born out in scripture. In Matthew 16:19, Christ gives us the keys to unlocking heaven: "and whatsoever thou shalt bind on earth shall be bound in heaven: and whatsoever thou shalt loose on earth shall be loosed in heaven" (KJV). The Message puts it this way:

> And that's not all. You will have complete and free access to God's kingdom, keys to open any and every door: no more barriers between heaven and earth, earth and

heaven. A yes on earth is a yes in heaven. A no on earth is a no in heaven.

Matthew 16:19 (The Message)

In essence, what Jesus is telling us is that words have power! Whatever we say sets the atmosphere for that very thing to happen. Hence, the power to unlocking heaven and receiving what God has for us, begins in our mouths.

We must learn Kingdom-speak. This means speaking the Word of God over our lives—even when it comes to fasting. In John 10:10, Christ promises us abundant living; it is Satan who seeks to take from us. So to say that fasting is about losing is to align that which is holy to that which is not. If Christ has promised us abundance, and if fasting is of Christ, then fasting should make us abundant. Therefore, if we are anticipating great results from our fast, then we must start to speak about fasting using the language of expectancy and abundance. Rather than saying, "I can't have chocolate for the next twenty-one days," choose to say instead, "For the next twenty-one days, I am choosing to drink more water and eat more fruits and vegetables." This choice of language shifts the focus to what you stand to gain versus what you will lose. By talking about what you will have more of during the fasting period, you add power to your fasting experience because now you are speaking a language of abundance. With each utterance, you partner with God to create the type of experience you speak about: "What you loose [or release] on earth, you loose [or release] in heaven" (Matthew 16:19, KJV).

By definition, fasting is a response to God's call to release or let go of some things. I choose to use these terms ("release" and "let go") because they are willful terms; they suggest that I am making a conscious choice. On the other hand, when we say we have "lost" something or "we have to give up" something, it means that something or someone else is doing the choosing for us, which weakens the power we have over that person or thing. Matthew 11:12 says, "The kingdom of heaven suffereth violence, and the violent take it by force" (KJV). We just discussed that access to the kingdom is available through our language.

Matthew 11:12 reveals that there are forces that will do whatever it takes to block our access to the kingdom. Therefore, we must meet these strongholds with even greater power than they exhibit. Thus, the camp of "can't," "won't," and "no" must be overcome by an even louder force of "can," "will," and "yes." Even in the *releasing* and the *letting go,* it is worthwhile to use language that keeps the kingdom available to us. Life and death lie in the power of our tongues. If we seek powerful results in our fast, then we must use language that gives power to our experience.

Rethinking the Purpose of Fasting

In Zechariah 7:5, God questions the fasts of the Jews: "When ye fasted and mourned in the fifth and seventh [month], even those seventy years, did ye at all fast unto me, [even] to me?" (KJV). In other words, God is asking if his chosen people were fasting for selfish reasons, or were they fasting for more of God and his power in their lives? We too must be mindful of why we fast unto God.

First off, let me say that fasting *out of desire* and fasting *because we feel pressured to* are two different things. If you are fasting because you feel you have to or are being forced to, then your chances of successful completion are greatly reduced. Think about it; we draw closer to that which we desire. Additionally, when it comes to those things that we *have* to do or we *must* do, we procrastinate or find something to redirect our attention. That shift in focus is why some people start their fast but end up quitting; one's own desire to fast must be evident if success is ultimately the goal.

However, having said this, allow me to say that we always have the opportunity to change our perspective. You may not have a great desire to fast now, but perhaps after reading this book you will begin to see the benefit that fasting poses for you, and it will become something that you want to do.

Additionally, fasting may not always change the results of potentially uncomfortable or negative situations, but it can prepare us for the future regardless of the outcome. Recall in Isaiah 58 that fasting may not always produce an immediate change in our circumstance but rather the ability to get through tough situations. In 2 Samuel 12, David fasts when his son becomes ill, and while his fasting does not prevent his son's death, verse eighteen indicates that when he hears the news of his son's death, he worships. While fasting may not always change our situations, it can change our outlook so that we are better able to deal with what has happened or is about to happen to us.

Queen Esther reveals the type of attitude that is useful to have while fasting. Esther, chapters four through seven, tells the story of how Haman, King Ahasuerus' son, orders to have all Jews killed because Mordecai (a Jew) refused to bow to him; however, it is after the people pray and fast that Esther gathers the courage to stand before the king unannounced to persuade him to change his decree. Normally, such an action would have meant death, but her fast emboldens her to do the unusual and unexpected. What is more impressive is that her fasting prepares her for any outcome. She commands Mordecai,

> [g]o, gather together all the Jews who are in Susa, and fast for me. Do not eat or drink for three days, night or day. I and my attendants will fast as you do. When this is done, I will go to the king, even though it is against the law. And if I perish, I perish.
>
> Esther 4:17 (NIV)

Esther's fasting frees her to accept God's will, even if the results are not favorable. In this instance, the outcome is what she and the Jews desire. Not only does Ahasuerus change his degree, but the very gallows that Haman has prepared for Mordecai and the Jews are used for his own hanging.

Fasting is not about quick fixes for longstanding problems, nor is it a barter-and- exchange with God. You cannot pay God for His favor. He owns the cattle on a thousand hills. In most instances, fasting alone will not make you richer, smarter, prettier, or healthier. However, what it will do is broaden and enrich your understanding of God and yourself. Purposeful fasting is about the deep soul-searching that is necessary to "work out your own salvation" (Philippians 2:12, KJV). Understand that this type of work is the most important work you will ever engage in because of its capacity to change every person and everything you touch. That is why fasting is so powerful, and that is why it is important that those who choose to fast do so for the right reasons.

Getting to Your Purpose (Leading)

Most of the time when fasting is mentioned in the Bible, people were preparing for a great work that God purposed them to do. In other words, they were preparing to lead. When we think of leaders, we think of people who are visible to the public. We think of politicians, preachers, doctors, and teachers. But in reality, we are all called to lead, which is to say we all have a purpose. If nothing else, we lead ourselves in how we think, feel, and act every day. So the fast that I am referring to does not leave out anyone. It does not discriminate by age or medical condition. Everyone able to make the decision to fast can be included. A gauge for readiness might be a person's ability to read this book and complete the visioning exercise in the next chapter.

Those who fast to understand their purpose seek to understand and know God's will for their lives. Sometimes we fast to recommit ourselves to living the kind of life God desires for us. For example, in Nehemiah 9-12 the people of God feel so responsible for the unproductive choices they have made after hearing the law read that they fast to recommit themselves to God and his commandments. With this said, fasting is for anyone desiring to lead a better life.

Fasting is essential to those who have assumed the responsibility of leading others. There is an old saying, "the higher the levels, the bigger the devils." With this said, it is no wonder that the first time we hear about Christ fasting he has an encounter with Satan himself. In Matthew 4, immediately after his baptism, Jesus is led into the desert by the Spirit to be tempted by Satan. To withstand the temptation, Jesus fasts for forty days and forty nights. Not only is Jesus able to resist Satan, but he outlasts him. Eventually, Satan leaves, and angels come to minister to Jesus. Let us remember that Christ fasted continuously throughout his ministry. It is this repeated practice of fasting that prepared him to do the extraordinary.

Likewise, those of us called to do the extraordinary must fast. In fact, the greater the work we are called to do, the more important it becomes to set aside time and space to get in the face of God. If Jesus, the very Son of God, found it necessary to fast, then who are we not to?

Ultimately, fasting is a quest to fulfill our purpose. It is an effort to find certainty in an ever-changing and uncertain world. Whether we fast to recommit our ourselves to God, to prepare us for difficult and challenging situations to make us open to God's will, or because we are beginning something new or are going against the grain to do the unexpected, fasting prepares us for the great work that awaits us.

Strategies for a Successful Fast

As you have just read in the previous chapter, fasting has the potential for changing ourselves, our families, and our communities. Change begins in us and can only happen when we are still enough to do the type of self-study that is necessary to bring about change. The fasting period is an ideal time for such reflection because although the term is called "fasting," it is meant to slow us down so that we can think, reflect, meditate, and pray to understand God's will for our lives.

This chapter begins your journey of self-reflection and earnestly taking a look at where you are spiritually and determining where it is you would like to be. I have provided three activities—two of which help you to examine what you truly desire for your life and identify what might be holding you back from achieving what you want. The third activity, the SMARTT-

FAST system, helps you to plan your fast thoughtfully so that you get the most out of your fast and increase your chances of completing it.

So that you receive the greatest benefit from these exercises, it will be important for you to work on them when you have time to think and are not distracted. You will need a pen or pencil to write down your thoughts. Be prepared to begin the journey of receiving the best God has in store for you!

Step 1: Create a Vision for Your Fast

The word "vision," in the sense that I am using it here, means to see what has not yet occurred. Proverbs 29:18 says "Where there is no vision, the people perish" (KJV). In order to complete any major task, you must first envision it. Visioning is a technique that allows you to picture how your life will be after obtaining your goal. The vision reminds us of the reason we fast and helps us to keep going throughout the fasting period. The following exercise will help you determine your purpose for fasting. It is important that you complete the exercise before you begin your fast so that you can see how fasting might benefit you on a personal level. This step is key in helping you make the shift from having to fast to wanting to fast.

Exercise 1: Visioning Exercise

Make a list of goals, dreams, projects, or tasks that you have not yet completed in your life or ministry or any challenges you have had for more than one year.

1. ______________________________

2. ______________________________

3. ______________________________

4. ______________________________

5. ______________________________

6. ______________________________

7. ______________________________

Which goal has presented the greatest challenge for you thus far?

____

Why is this goal important to you or your ministry?

____

____

____

____

Now, let's imagine what your life or ministry will look like after you have accomplished your goal:

What are you doing and who is with you?

____

____

____

____

How much fun are you having?

____

How are you or your ministry different:

Physically?

____

____

Financially?

____

____

Spiritually?

____

____

What impact are you having in the lives of those around you (e.g. your family? your church? your community?)

____

____

Now, continue to imagine *what* (not how) you will feel once you have accomplished your goal.

____

____

Your answer to this last question is important because it points to what you truly desire. It is the place of opportunity for God to begin to do a mighty work in you. The key word here is "in" because only when you begin to work on the "you" from the inside can you begin to handle what God has in store for you on the outside.

Now copy the word you just wrote (the word that describes how you will feel once you've accomplished your goal) in the blank below.

My purpose for fasting is to be more ________ ____________________________ for the Kingdom of God.

Whatever word you have placed in this blank describes what it is you truly desire and is an opportunity for God to begin to perform a wonderful work in you. It is God's opportunity to deposit more of His qualities in you.

Based on the word you have written above, make a list of what has been holding you or your ministry back from having what God truly desires for you.

1. ____

2. ____

3. ____

4. ____

5. ____

6. ____

7. ____

8. ____

9. ____

10.____

If you were doubtful about fasting before, this list has now given you several reasons to fast. It indicates the thoughts and behaviors that need to be emptied out of you to make room for the purpose God has called you to.

Exercise 2: Create a Vision Board

Another way to capture the purpose for your fast is to create a vision board. This activity can be especially fun for those who are artistic or visual. It is also a great way to invite youth to start thinking about their dreams, goals, and values. This conversation can then lead to future discussions about their gifts and talents and how they see themselves using them in service to others. You can increase the enjoyment by creating individual vision boards in a group setting or by having a vision board party. Afterward, everyone can share his or her vision board with the group. Prayers can then be made over each other's dreams and goals. Vision boards can also be quite effective for groups working on a collective vision. That is, one vision board can reflect the goals and values of an entire group.

I created a vision board a couple of years ago, and it still hangs in the wall of my office as a constant reminder of who it is I aspire to be and how I choose to live my life. Proverbs 23:7 expresses the sentiment that we become what we think and believe. The vision board becomes a visual representation of our thoughts and beliefs and provides the motivation to bring what is on paper into fruition. The act of creating the vision board makes our thoughts and beliefs tangible.

I remember watching an episode on *Oprah* a couple of years ago that featured the story of Dr. Tererai Trent, an African woman who was in an oppressive marriage but had hopes for a better life. She wrote her dreams on a piece of paper, dug a hole in the ground and buried them there. Each time one of her dreams would materialize, she would add another to the list and place it in its new home with the other items. This woman finally realized her dream of escaping her abusive marriage, has since gone on to obtain her PhD, and has dreams of building a school to help educate the women in her native country, Zimbabwe.[23] My board has worked in the same fashion for me.

Even though I do not look at my board every day, the intention that led me to create it is buried deep in my heart. And it is that same intention that has allowed me to begin seeing what is represented there manifesting in my life.

My board has four major themes: family, financial freedom, spirituality, and destiny. The one word that summarizes everything on the board and that holds the greatest value for me is the word "FREE," written in fat, orange letters, situated in its rightful place at the top of the page. Every day I experience myself becoming freer: judgment-free, debt-free, worry-free, fat-free, drama-free, spiritually free.

Even the picture of my dream home located in the lower right corner expresses my goal of freedom. It is set off peacefully in the woods, nestled among trees, an extension of nature almost. I envision myself stepping out onto the porch, gazing into the crisp, blue sky with cup of coffee in hand. This is where I greet God in the mornings, this sanctuary of absolute quiet and peace. I close my eyes, take in the welcoming breeze, and gaze upon the fresh, fallen leaves. I breathe in deeply, then exhale, smiling at the thought that I am here at last, where I am meant to be—home.

The largest of my goals has yet to be attained, but the expression of what I desire for my life on paper somehow makes it more tangible, undeniable even. The items on this board are more than pictures and words on paper; they are the Creator's promises to me that I hold out my life to receive.

A vision board is basically a collection of pictures, words, and phrases that serve as a constant reminder of what it is you desire. Throughout the Old Testament, the Israelites erected stone monuments as physical remembrances of what God had done for them (see Exodus 17 for example). A vision board has a similar purpose in that it is a constant reminder of what we are expecting from God, and after we have received it, it becomes a reminder of what God has done.

The visioning exercise on the previous page can serve as a useful starting point for your vision board since it provides you the opportunity to think about and write down what it is you truly desire from God.

To create a vision board, you need the following:

1. old magazines or newspapers that you no longer tend to use
2. favorite quotes or scriptures

3. personal photos, if you wish
4. scissors
5. glue stick
6. poster board

Step 1: Using the magazines or newspapers, generously cut out pictures, words, or phrases that truly resonate with you or that speak to who it is you would like to be. You can also use your computer to print out an appropriate scripture or meaningful photos that help express what you truly want for your life.

Step 2: Arrange the photos and words on the poster board until they fill the entire board. Since the vision board is personal, you may choose to place a picture of you and your family in the center of the board. Once you have arranged the words and photos in the format you like, use the glue stick to adhere them to the board.

Step 3: Place the board in a strategic location so that you can look at it often as a reminder of what you desire for your life or ministry.

Step 2: Plan a SMARTT-FAST

One of the reasons people have difficulty fasting is because of lack of planning. For this reason, I have developed the SMARTT-FAST system—a planning guide for your fast that helps to greatly improve your chances of success. A SMARTT-FAST is:

S=Specific

M=rightly-Motivated

A=Achievable

R=Realistic

T=Type-specific

T=Time-specific

F=Focused on Finishing for your Future

A=Accountable

S=Stretchable

T=prepared for the Test and the Testimony

Answer the questions after each description item to help you plan a SMARTT-FAST.

S=Specific

I cannot emphasize this point enough: every spiritual fast has a God-appointed purpose. Know what you are fasting for. If you have completed the vision activity, then you have already identified what this is. Write it in the space below. If you have not already done so, go back and complete the vision activity at the beginning of this chapter so that you are clear about why you are fasting.

1. My purpose for fasting is to be more ______________________________ for the kingdom of God. (Whatever word you have placed in this blank describes what it is you truly desire and is an opportunity for God to begin and perform a wonderful work in you. It is God's opportunity to deposit more of His qualities in you.)

2. What might you need more of you in your life to achieve this quality?

____

____

3. What might you need less of in your life to achieve this quality?

M=Motive

James 4:3 says, "When you ask, you do not receive, because you ask with wrong motives, that you may spend what you get on your pleasures" (NIV). Remember that the goal of a spiritual fast is ultimately to help others. The following questions will help you to identify a right motive for fasting.

Who, besides yourself, will benefit from your fast once it is over?

____

____

____

____

How will the thing you are fasting for glorify God?

____

____

____

____

A=Achievable

Consider if the type of fast you have chosen is achievable for you. People are motivated by just the *thought* that they can achieve a task, so choosing a fast that you *think* you can complete is important. If this is your very first time fasting, perhaps fasting for twenty-one days on water alone is not the ideal place for you to start. In fact, most advocates of fasting agree that those fasting for the first time begin with a 24-hour fast and then gradually build to a longer fast.[24]

Knowing the type of fast you have chosen and the length of your fast are important for deciding whether or not the fast is achievable. So turn over a couple of pages and answer questions regarding the type of fast you will engage in as well as the length of your fast. Once you have completed those sections, answer the questions below:

Based on the *type* of fast you have chosen and the length of *time* you have devoted for this fast, to what extent is your chosen fast achievable?

____

____

____

____

On a scale from one to ten, with one being not likely at all and ten being definitely likely, how likely is it that you will complete your chosen fast?

____

If your answer is less than ten, name one thing you can do to increase the possibility of you finishing.

____

____

R=Realistic

Not only is it important that the type of fast you engage in is achievable, but it is also important that your requests of God are realistic. Consider your readiness to receive from God.

How prepared are you to receive what you are asking God for?

____

What thoughts, beliefs, and plans must be in place in order for you to have what you want?

____

____

____

T=Type

Remember that the purpose for fasting is to let go of whatever may interfere with you hearing from God. Knowing what to release is important since your decision has the potential to move you closer to what it is you desire. Therefore, when thinking about what you are willing to let go of, consider taking a break from behaviors that have kept you from your goal thus far. You have already created such a list in the visioning exercise at the beginning of this chapter. One of the items on the list might be anger. In this case, it might be helpful to separate yourself from certain people or activities that create anger in you. This might mean fasting from television or talking on the phone.

In the space below, write down what you are willing to let go of for your fast.

____

____

____

____

How will this willful sacrifice ultimately help you achieve *who* it is you want to be?

____

____

____

____

T=Time

How might you hear God's voice calling you to fast? Lynne Baab, suggests the following:

> Sometimes we will hear something-in a sermon, from a friend, in a Bible class-that nudges us toward a particular fast. Sometimes a growing conviction in our hearts, a kind of inner voice, urges us to fast. Sometimes in prayer or reflection we become aware of a growing imbalance in our lives. At times we long for a deeper experience of God, and fasting seems like the best way to respond to that longing.[25]

She goes on to write that tough decisions and choices also lead us to fast.[26] Whenever you feel the urge the fast, follow it. It is God's way of getting your attention to speak directly to you.

Once you are clear that you have been called to fast, how long will you fast? Will it be one day? A week? A month? What you are fasting for will usually determine the length of your fast. Nevertheless, having said this, know that the time of your fast is up to you and God. The length you choose may increase over time. You may start off fasting three hours a day and gradually build toward eight hours. What is important is that you set aside time to focus on hearing from God. Consider also how you will use the time that you've set apart. Will you spend it reading God's Word? Listening to gospel music? Meditating? Engaging in worship and praise? Consider also what time of day you will set aside for just you and God. Choose a time of day where you are least likely to be distracted. For me, that time is between six and seven in the morning before anyone else in my house arises.

How long do you plan on fasting?

____

When will you set aside time for just you and God during your fast?

____

How do you plan to use that time?

____

____

____

____

F=Finishing for your Future

Genesis 25:20-34 provides a wonderful story of why you should not quit during your fasting season. Twins at birth, Esau, the eldest brother, sold all the rights and privileges of being the firstborn to his younger brother, Jacob, for a bowl of soup. This was not an equal trade-off by any stretch. Being the first-born carried with it many privileges. Upon the death of his father, the eldest son would not only be given authority over his entire family, including his siblings and their wives, unmarried daughters and grandchildren,[27] but the eldest son was also given a double-portion of land, property, and wealth.[28] Because Esau, a hunter by trade, was hungry at that moment, he accepted the bribe of his brother Jacob to sell him all the privileges of his birthright for a bowl of soup. Now, I know if you're like me, you're thinking to yourself, *Really, Esau, for a bowl of soup?* But because Esau was impatient and impulsive, because he could not see beyond that moment, he gave up all that was promised to him. Verse 34 says that after eating the soup, he "despised his birthright," which is to say that he was filled with guilt and regret. This momentary lapse in judgment would lead to long-term consequences that would affect him for a lifetime.

We've already examined in Isaiah 58 the promises of God that await us when we truly fast unto Him. At this point, you've already created a vision of what your life will be like after the fasting period has ended; you may have even created your own vision board that serves as a physical reminder of God's presence and promises in your life. Would you dare give all of that up for food, the internet, social media, or whatever you have chosen to willingly surrender during your fast? On the other side of the fast lies your destiny, your future, your inheritance. Isn't it worth much, much more? Whatever the nature of your fast, I implore you, in the words of the psalmist to "Wait on the LORD, and keep his way, and he shall exalt thee to inherit the land" (Psalm 37:3a, KJV).

Sometimes fasting will become difficult, and you will want to give up. At these times, keep your goal in the forefront of your mind and the impact of fasting on your future. What will you have to look forward to? Also consider what aspects of your fast you will carry over into the future. Since the Daniel Fast has made me a more thoughtful shopper, I am an avid reader of labels now, and I have limited my family's intake of preservatives, fats, and sugars. As a result, we are healthier—a benefit that is certainly worth keeping.

What do you have to look forward to once you complete your fast?

____

____

____

____

What parts of your fasting experience do you plan to keep?

____

____

____

____

A=Accountability

Even though you may be involved in a corporate fast involving a lot of people, it is wise to have one or two partners that you can answer directly to regarding the progress of your fast. This person believes in and supports what you are doing and is available to encourage you to keep going. Ideally, this person is also fasting and can share the experience with you—both its challenges and its rewards. Scot McKnight writes:

> Any community that doesn't tolerate normal struggles with fasting or [doesn't] permit flexibility will damage its own witness, and the spiritual freedom of its members will be constricted by legalism.[29]

Make sure that the fasting community of which you are a part is a supportive one that has one goal: to love you to the finish line.

You can decide up front how often you would like to check in with each other. Depending on the length of the fast, it may be daily or weekly. What is important is knowing that you have a reassuring presence on which you can rely.

Who is your accountability partner(s) for this fast?

____

____

____

How often will you check in with this person(s)?

____

Who will make the call to check in?

____

How do you plan to support those who are accountable to you? (Some of the ways you can do this are through confidentiality, non-judgment, active listening, and availability).

____

____

____

____

S=Stretch yourself

Fasting is a time of great expectation, so if we are to receive greatly, we must be willing to give more of ourselves. If you are used to reading God's Word for five minutes a day, stretch it to ten minutes. Do more than what is normal so that you give yourself more opportunity to hear from God.

What are you willing to do more of that is not a part of your regular routine during this period of fasting that will draw you closer to God?

____

____

____

____

T=Test and Testimony

Do not be surprised if you are tested during this period of fasting and the time following your fast. One of the tests you may face is Satan causing you to doubt what God has spoken or promised you. That is why it is important to keep a journal during the fasting period. Journaling allows you to recall with confidence what God has said to you directly as it relates to your destiny. For this reason, I have prepared a journal for you to record each day's insights and miracles over a twenty-one day period in the next chapter. You may take a scripture or an insight and place it in a location that you can refer to regularly and easily. One of my insights still hangs above the desk in my office. It reads "Today, I will trust God." It continues to serve as a constant reminder of God's faithfulness to me during challenging times. It will be important to rely on such insights to guide your actions as you move forward. As God's plans for your life become clearer, prepare to share your testimony with others.

What will be your strategy for continuing your fast when you are tested?

____

____

____

____

With whom will you share your testimony?

____

____

Recognizing, Preparing, and Developing the Leader in You

This chapter consists of a twenty-one day guide that prepares you to do the inner work necessary to develop into an effective leader. The guide is divided into three phases or sections, each consisting of inspirational songs that can be accessed through YouTube or downloaded on your iPod, scriptures, journal activities, and pro-active prayers that address specific aspects of self-development and leadership.

Phase I focuses on your identity in Christ. It is this understanding that ultimately leads you to your purpose. When you understand that you are connected to God through Christ, you begin to identify with your Creator and develop the desire to create—just as He created you. Phase two takes you on a journey of self-examination that will enable you to examine and address those beliefs, attitudes, and behaviors that have kept you from taking the lead in certain areas of your life. It is true that until we begin to lead ourselves, we will remain ill-equipped to lead anyone else. Phase three prepares you to lead yourself, your family, and community by focusing on those qualities that make you an effective leader.

I realize that some fasts may be longer or shorter than the time that is designated here. In these instances, feel free to customize the contents to meet your specific needs. For example, you may find that you need to spend more than a day on a single topic, thus extending your fast beyond twenty-one days. For times when you are led to fast for shorter periods, you may choose a single topic that speaks to your situation and then focus only on that area. What is important is that you take the time to listen to what God is saying to you regardless of the length of your fast. Because fasting familiarizes us with the voice of God inside of us, you will know whether it is the appropriate time to continue your fast or to end it.

Phase One: Knowing Myself, My God, and My Purpose

Day One

"My Identity"

Inspirational Song: "I Know Who I Am" by Lakewood

Meditative Scriptures: 2 Corinthians 5: 14-21; Ephesians 1

In what way does this scripture speak to your situation?

____

____

____

What is your new insight, revelation, or miracle of the day?

What are you now led to do as a result?

Prayer: Thank you, heavenly Father, that at each moment I can decide who it is I want to be. Through Jesus, I can begin my life anew. Today, I choose to be like You and to live in the freedom that Your salvation offers. With this new identity comes a new way of looking at myself, others, and my experiences. With You all things are possible. Amen.

Day Two

"My Relationship with God"

Inspirational Song: "Nothing Can Separate Me" by Lakewood and "More" by Cece Winans

Meditative Scriptures: Colossians 3: 1-17; Philippians 3

In what way does this scripture speak to your situation?

____

____

____

____

What is your new insight, revelation, or miracle of the day?

____

____

____

____

____

What are you now led to do as a result?

____

____

____

____

Prayer: Lord God, thank You for my new life with You. Today, I pursue compassion, kindness, humility, persistence, orderliness, self-control, forgiveness, peace, and love. I commit to showing others who You are with my every thought, word, and deed. By placing my focus on You, I make You larger in my life. Be glorified, Father. Amen.

Day Three

"My Choices"

Inspirational Song: "I Choose to Worship" by Wess Morgan

Meditative Scriptures: Proverbs 16: 1-9; Jeremiah 29: 10-14

In what way does this scripture speak to your situation?

____

____

____

____

What is your new insight, revelation, or miracle for the day?

____

____

What are you now led to do as a result?

Prayer: Lord God, thank You for the plans You have for me. Thank You for placing me at the right place at the right time for Your purpose. I surrender my work, my hopes, and my dreams to You. Help me to choose what truly is good for me and what is pleasing in Your sight. Amen.

Day Four

"My Creativity /Spiritual Gifts"

Inspirational Song: "Available" by Melinda Watts

Meditative Scripture: 1 Corinthians 12

In what way does this scripture speak to your situation?

____

____

____

____

What is your new insight, revelation, or miracle of the day?

____

____

____

What are you now led to do as a result?

Prayer: Thank You, God, for the gifts You have given me that reveal Your power in my life. And because it is You who have given me these gifts, I am important and significant, whether I am standing out front or working quietly behind the scenes. Thank You for using my gifts along with the gifts of others to carry out Your will. Through You, I know that I can do *all* things, and because of You, I am already good enough. Amen.

Day Five

"My Purpose/Calling"

Inspirational Song: "Yes" by Shekinah Glory and "Prophetic Medley/The High Place" by LaShun Pace

Meditative Scripture: Romans 12

In what way does this scripture speak to your situation?

____

____

____

____

What is your new insight, revelation, or miracle of the day?

____

____

What are you now led to do as a result?

Prayer: Father God, thank You for seeing and bringing out the best in me. I desire to see myself as clearly as You see me. I take my eyes off of others and fix them squarely on You. Today, I focus on my purpose and what You have called me to be, and I offer it as a sacrifice to You. Direct me to institutions and organizations that help me carry out Your will for my life. Amen.

Phase Two: Doing the Inner Work that Prepares Me to Lead

Day Six

"Addressing Fear and Worry"

Inspirational Songs: "Safe" by Phil Wickham and "Resting on His Promise" by Youthful Praise

Meditative Scripture: Philippians 4: 4-13

In what way does this scripture speak to your situation?

____

____

What is your new insight, revelation, or miracle for the day?

What are you now led to do as a result?

Prayer: Oh, Lord, thank You for loving me and for caring for me. And because You love me, I never have to fret or worry. Help me to make the most of what I have right now. Deliver me from need so that I am content in any situation. Father, I release all that is not meant for me and embrace all that You have in store. I hope and trust in You. Amen.

Day Seven

"Addressing Past Hurt"

Inspirational Songs: "The Lifter" by Ted Winn and "He Has His Hands on You" by Marvin Sapp

Meditative Scriptures: Psalms 37; Matthew 18: 12-35

In what way does this scripture speak to your situation?

____

____

____

____

What is your new insight, revelation, or miracle for the day?

____

____

What are you now led to do as a result?

Prayer: Oh Lord, thank You for Your tender mercies toward me. Help me to be forgiving, righteous, truthful, faithful, and peaceful toward others as You are to me. When others have done me harm, help me not to respond in kind but to trust in You and do good, instead. I understand that when I demonstrate Your qualities, I release Your mighty powers to work through me and for me. I praise You right now for a renewed mind and for mended relationships. Amen.

Day Eight

"Addressing Temptation"

Inspirational Songs: "My Desire" by Tyrone Powell and "Get Back Up" by TobyMac

Meditative Scriptures: James 4; 2 Corinthians 6: 14-2 Corinthians 7:1; Ephesians 6: 10-20

In what way does this scripture speak to your situation?

____

____

____

____

What is your new insight, revelation, or miracle for the day?

____

____

What are you now led to do as a result?

Prayer: Father God, thank You for giving me the power to face any temptation that comes into my life. You are greater than the forces of this world that attempt to hold me back from reaching my full potential. Give me the strength to overcome any temptation by being prepared, getting help, reading your word, praying, and being accountable to others. Amen.

Day Nine

"Addressing Time Management"

Inspirational Song: "Move" by Mercyme and "Get Up" by Mary Mary

Meditative Scriptures: Romans 13: 11-14; 1 Corinthians 7: 29-35; Ecclesiastes 3

In what way does this scripture speak to your situation?

____

____

____

____

What is your new insight, revelation, or miracle for the day?

____

____

What are you now led to do as a result?

Prayer: Dear Lord, thank You for the time that is mine to enjoy. Help me to clearly understand my purpose so that I am not wasting one minute but am living my dreams and doing what I love. I seek Your wisdom to know the right time to speak or act. Amen.

Day Ten

"Addressing Finances"

Inspirational Songs: "New Season" by Israel and New Breed and "Over" by Youth for Christ

Meditative Scriptures: Psalms 37; Luke 12: 13-34

In what way does this scripture speak to your situation?

____

____

____

____

What is your new insight, revelation, or miracle of the day?

____

____

____

____

What are you now led to do as a result?

____

____

____

____

Prayer: Father God, thank You for meeting my every need. I take comfort in the fact that You've never allowed me to experience anything that You did not give me the strength, wisdom, or courage to get through. For these reasons, I will not worry about my financial situation, but instead I will rest in You. Give right focus to my life. Help me to invest my time, talent, and money to that which brings glory to You. Take joy in my life and my life choices. Amen.

Day Eleven

"Addressing Fun and Enjoyment"

Inspirational Song: "Freedom" by Eddie James and "Stand Out" by Tye Tribbett & GA

Meditative Scriptures: Ecclesiastes 2: 24-26; Ecclesiastes 5: 18-20; Ecclesiastes 6; Ecclesiastes 9: 7-10

In what way does this scripture speak to your situation?

What is your new insight, revelation, or miracle of the day?

What are you now led to do as a result?

Prayer: Dear God, thank You for the life You have given me to enjoy. Today, I make the most of my life by following my dreams and passions. I invest my time in those activities that truly make my life worth living. I strive for a meaningful existence, living freely in each moment, being open to any outcome You desire for me. Amen.

Day Twelve

"Addressing Health/Aging"

Inspirational Songs: "Walking" and "Slow Walking" by Mary Mary

Meditative Scriptures: Psalm 90; 1 Corinthians 10: 23-31

In what way does this scripture speak to your situation?

____

____

____

____

What is your new insight, revelation, or miracle of the day?

____

____

____

____

What are you now led to do as a result?

____

____

____

____

Prayer: Father God, I thank You for my life and health. Thank You for the length of days You have given me to do Your will. You have created me to do a great work, and I will not endanger that work by doing harm to my body. I can only give You my best if I am choosing those foods and activities that increase my chances for healthy living and long life. I commit to those choices that allow me to glorify You in this body. Amen.

Phase Three: Developing the Mind-set of a Leader

Day Thirteen

"What It Takes to Lead Others"

Inspirational Song: "Light in Me" by Brandon Heath and "Champion" by Darwin Hobbs

Meditative Scriptures: 1 Peter 5:1-11; Proverbs 16: 10-33: 1 Timothy 3: 1-13

In what way does this scripture speak to your situation?

____

____

What is your new insight, revelation, or miracle for the day?

What are you now led to do as a result?

Prayer: Lord, I thank You for those You have placed in my care to lead. I thank You for the work You have called me to, and I do it willfully. Help me to lead honestly but gently and to live out my beliefs wisely without fear. Let my actions speak louder than my words. I hope and believe in You. Amen.

Day Fourteen

"What It Takes to Lead My Family"

Inspirational Song: "Peace and Favor" by Kurt Carr and the Kurt Carr Singers

Meditative Scriptures: Proverbs 13:22-14:1-11; Colossians 3:18-4:6

In what way does this scripture speak to your situation?

____

____

____

____

What is your new insight, revelation, or miracle of the day?

____

____

What are you now led to do as a result?

Prayer: Thank You, God, for my family and for the specific role(s) I play. Help me to be the person You have called me to be so that I may offer my best to my family. Today, I lay aside all thoughts and behaviors that have caused hurt and pain to myself and my loved ones, and I embrace those thoughts and behaviors that lend themselves to growth and harmony. Today, I will focus on that which truly matters. It is in Your blessed name I pray. Amen.

Day Fifteen

“What it Takes to Lead My Single/Married Life”

Inspirational Songs: “You Hold My World/How He Loves” by Israel Houghton and “Nothing Can Separate Me” by Lakewood

Meditative Scriptures: 1 Corinthians 7: 32-40; Ecclesiastes 4: 7-12 (for singles)

1 Corinthians 7: 10-17; I Corinthians 13 (for married couples)

In what way does this scripture speak to your situation?

____

____

____

____

____

What is your new insight, revelation, or miracle of the day?

What are you now led to do as a result?

Prayer for singles: Dear God, I thank You for my single status and for the freedom that it allows. Thank You for the time You have given me to have fun and to do Your work. It is Your work that fulfills and completes me and assures me that I am enough. I am content no matter what state I am in—whether I choose to remain single or whether I choose to marry. Either way, I will use my life to glorify You. Amen.

Prayer for married couples: Father God, thank You for the spouse that I have chosen. Help us to demonstrate love in our marriage by never giving up, by putting each other first, by being calm when we disagree, and by forgiving easily. Today, we look for the very best in each other. We know that together we can do anything! We place our faith and trust in You. Amen.

Day Sixteen

"What It Takes to Lead My Community"

Inspirational Song: "Cover the Earth" and "Everywhere that I Go" by Israel Houghton

Meditative Scriptures: James 3: 13-18; Matthew 28: 16-20; Acts 1:8

In what way does this scripture speak to your situation?

____

____

____

____

What is your new insight, revelation, or miracle of the day?

____

____

What are you now led to do as a result?

Prayer: Lord, thank You for the work that carries me beyond the walls of my home and church and into the larger community. I am grateful for the opportunity to share Your gospel and inspire change in others. Help me always to see the mission and the greater good of the community over my own private agenda. Amen.

Day Seventeen

"How an Effective Leader Communicates"

Inspirational Song: "We Speak to Nations" by Lakewood

Meditative Scriptures: James 3: 3-18; 1 Corinthians 14

In what way does this scripture speak to your situation?

____

____

____

____

What is your new insight, revelation, or miracle of the day?

____

____

____

____

What are you now led to do as a result?

____

____

____

____

Prayer: Father God, thank You for the gift of language and for the power to bless and inspire others with my words. Help me to demonstrate wisdom in my words and actions and to be a testimony to others of Your love and grace. I give You glory, honor, and praise. Amen.

Day Eighteen

"How an Effective Leader Thinks"

Inspirational Song: "Expect the Great" by Jonathan Nelson and "Faithful to Believe" by Byron Cage

Meditative Scripture: Philippians 4: 4-20

In what way does this scripture speak to your situation?

____

____

____

____

What is your new insight, revelation, or miracle of the day?

____

____

____

____

What are you now led to do as a result?

____

____

____

____

Prayer: Father God, thank You for seeing the best in me and for believing the best about me. I commit to doing the same with others. Help me to think, see, believe, and speak only that which is good about those with whom I live, work, and play. I recognize the power of my thoughts, so help me to think, see, believe, and speak only that which is good over my own life and situation. I know that while I rely on Your Word to strengthen me, I can do anything. I place my faith and trust in You. Amen.

Day Nineteen

"How an Effective Leader Handles Desire"

Inspirational Song: "I Desire More" by Crystal Aikin and "Empty Me" by William Murphy

Meditative Scriptures: Proverbs 23; Hebrews 13:5-6; Luke 12: 22-34

In what way does this scripture speak to your situation?

____

____

____

____

What is your new insight, revelation, or miracle of the day?

____

____

____

____

What are you now led to do as a result?

____

____

____

____

Prayer: Thank You, oh omniscient and omnipotent God. You know all about me, and You are all powerful. For this reason, I know I can be carefree in You. Today, I choose to focus on You and Your promises and not on my present circumstance. I know I have more than enough because I have You. Today, I place everything I value in your capable hands. I devote every thought and action to You. Amen.

Day Twenty

"How an Effective Leader Handles Opposition"

Inspirational Songs: "Nothing Can Separate Me" by Lakewood and "Hold On" by TobyMac

Meditative Scriptures: Ephesians 6: 10-20; Matthew 10: 16-28

In what way does this scripture speak to your situation?

____

____

____

____

What is your new insight, revelation, or miracle of the day?

____

____

What are you now led to do as a result?

Prayer: Dear God, thank You for the calling on my life. I realize that sometimes what You are calling me to do may go against manmade traditions. At these times, give me the courage to obey You, even if the direction in which I am being led is unfamiliar or unpopular. I place my life in Your hands. Amen.

Day Twenty-One

"How an Effective Leader Perseveres"

Inspirational Songs: "Stay Strong" by the Newsboys and "I Shall Live" by Jason Nelson

Meditative Scripture: 2 Corinthians 6

In what way does this scripture speak to your situation?

____

____

____

____

What is your new insight, revelation, or miracle for the day?

____

____

___

___

What are you now led to do as a result?

___

___

___

___

Prayer: Heavenly Father, thank You for this work that calls me to be orderly and prepared, for I realize that it is in the details of my life that I can most clearly reflect You. I open my heart to live boldly and freely before You. Help me to live a life worthy of following and give me the strength to stay at my post and to keep going—no matter what happens. Amen.

Coming Off of Your Fast

I remember waking up the last day of my fast feeling quite sad. I had successfully reached the end and had started to doubt my purpose again. I questioned this book and everything God had told me over the past twenty days. "Who was I kidding?" I asked myself. "So many books are being written nowadays by people already established in the ministry and by those with their own TV programs. Why would anyone pick up my book?" Here it was, the final day of my fast, and I had expected to be full in God, but on the contrary, I felt quite empty.

Then I remembered how Satan tempted Jesus near the end of his fast. It was also right before the start of his ministry. The very first trick Satan tried to pull was to question Jesus's relationship with God. "*If* you are the son of God, tell these stones to become bread" (Matthew 4:3, NIV, italics added by author). From this scripture, I realized that Satan was trying to do the same thing to me. He wanted me to question my relationship with God and His plan and purpose in my life.

In that moment of doubt, my mind went back to day six of my fast. It had come in the mail again—the bright yellow envelope with my name scrawled in blue letters as if someone had taken the time to write directly to me. I have to give it to them. The producers of the Publisher's Clearing House Sweepstakes really know how to make you feel special. The envelope read that it was *guaranteed* that I was one of a select number that would go into the pool of candidates eligible to win one million dollars for the rest of my life! In one month, my life circumstances could be changed forever. I had saved all the other envelopes as a reminder to myself to log online to enter. I'm not much of a gambler, but again, I was desperate. The last time they sent out an entry, I logged on faithfully every day to register my name to receive the winnings; I was hopeful for anything. I would scroll through the list of daily winners, and at times I'd see folks' names from Maryland—no one I ever knew, of course—but they were in the same state, so that meant that I stood a chance of winning something! Like the man Jesus found at the pool of Bethesda, waiting for someone to put him in, I waited for someone to draw my name to change my fate.

I had not submitted the entry, but I kept it in full view on my kitchen island so that I would not forget to submit it after the fast. It's funny how God knows us. Trust had been one of the areas of my life that God was working on, and He wanted all of me. As I looked at the entry, I heard Him ask, "Me or them?"

"What, God?" I replied sheepishly, knowing full well what He meant.

"Will you trust me today for your future and for your destiny, or will you continue to throw your pearls before swine?" I understood fully. The minutes I devoted each day to completing the registration form to enter my name could have been time devoted to writing my book and to understanding how God wanted to use me. I trusted God, but PCH would be my back-up plan. That moment was a test to believe God fully and to know that He was large enough to contain all my hopes and dreams. I could continue to gamble, hoping that my name would be drawn, or I could use the gifts that God had entrusted me and thereby take control of my own destiny.

As I tossed my PCH Sweepstakes entry in the trash and cast my cares on Him, I responded, "Yes, Lord, I will trust you."

As I flashed back to the present, those words echoed again in my head. I repeated them out loud again for impact. "Yes, Lord, I will trust you." For the next four months, I kept my promise to God. I arose at six every morning and continued to write. By May, I had completed most of the book and was making one of many final revisions. My plan was to self-publish the book because I had read somewhere that that is how most writers get started nowadays, but one day on a whim, I decided to submit my manuscript to Tate Publishing. I chose Tate because they are a Christian publishing company whose values aligned with my own, and so I figured, why not? As I read more about them, I discovered they only accepted about three percent of the thousands of manuscripts submitted to them. I thought to myself, *Wow, that's a very small percentage,* but I had nothing to lose, so I downloaded the draft I was working on and submitted it anyway. I had no expectations. I clicked the submit button and walked away.

Almost three months later, while on another fast, out of the blue, I received an email from one of Tate's representatives stating that my manuscript was being reviewed and I would receive notification of whether or not it had been accepted in a few weeks. Again, I thought nothing of it. At this point, I was still revising as God kept speaking to me about what to add and change in the text. The next day, I received a phone call from the same representative who had emailed me the night before. She was excited about my submission and offered to let Tate publish my book. I was stunned. Although I remained *amazingly* composed when speaking to her, after we hung up, I leaped in the air with a shout. "Yes!" This was better than any sweepstakes. God had opened the door to my destiny. It took Him eight months to do what I had not done in four years since completing my dissertation, and He did it all in grand style. Here I was—a first-time author who had submitted her first manuscript to a major publishing company and received a call within three short months. Indeed, God is amazing.

I share this story with you because I realize that when your fast is over, many of you will hesitate to begin or even complete the work God has called you to do. Satan will start to work on you, and you will question your ability and whether you are good enough, smart enough, or even ready to go the places where God is leading you. That's why this book is so powerful. It was co-written by me and you. The numerous journal exercises were designed to remind you of God's promises to you and to equip you with action plans to carry them out. After the fast is over, revisit your journal pages. Recall how you felt when you wrote them, and then go on to claim what is yours in Jesus's name.

Celebrate!

Ending the fast is an important moment and is one that should not be taken lightly. It is an opportunity to capture the excitement of completion and to look to the future. If you have been fasting with your friends or church members, consider having a testimony service where participants share their insights or miracles. Invite participants to share scriptures or songs that proved valuable to them during the fast. If you were on the Daniel Fast, have a recipe-exchange and serve your favorite Daniel Fast meals. The event might even be reflective. It may involve participants answering one or more of the following questions:

- What major revelations did the fast reveal to you about your purpose?
- What major discoveries did you make about yourself?
- What major discoveries did you make about your God?
- What surprised you most during this period?
- What practices of this fast will you take into the future?
- What are your next steps, now that you have completed the fast?

Whatever activities you engage in to celebrate the end of your fast, use that moment to get you and others excited about the new work that God has called you to.

The New Work

After the celebration begins the planning and putting into effect of all that you have learned and discovered about your purpose, your God, and yourself. This can be the challenging part because the work itself can be lonely. But go on with confidence, knowing that what

God has revealed to you is real and that the work that awaits you was tailor-made just for you. Think about who you are now prepared to lead and how.

During the fasting period, you may have discovered what your special gifts and talents are. If this is the case, search out opportunities to develop and use them. You may also have found opportunities to lead yourself better in specific areas in your life such as your health or finances. If this is the case, then go about developing strategies that will help you give your best physically or financially. At another level, the fast may have revealed ways to improve your relationship with others. On the day designated for me to focus on my marriage, I became excited because I anticipated what God would have me to tell my husband. (I had a whole list of suggestions). But the scriptures encouraged me to examine more closely who *I* was in our marriage and to reflect on the changes *I* could make to be a more supportive spouse.

Furthermore, if you were already in a leadership position outside your home, consider how your approach to leadership will be different. Then start developing strategies that will make you more effective in your current role. Set new goals and new action plans for yourself. Determine what people and resources you will need to consult to help you reach your goals. Most importantly, remember all that God has spoken to you during this time of fasting and allow His promises to propel you toward your purpose.

Leading Others to Fast Successfully

Throughout this book, I have spent a great deal of time honing in on the individual aspects of fasting. In other words, most of what has been written here has been geared towards the "pew." Now, I'd like to address the pulpit by providing suggestions to leaders who may, after reading this book, feel called to introduce purposeful fasting in churches, individual ministries, or small groups. Together, the six tips provided here focus on specific ways to make fasting relevant, focused, meaningful, and even fun. More strategies for conducting group fasts can be found in the facilitator's guide for this book at www.highcallcoaching.com.

Have a clearly stated purpose or reason for calling the fast.

Richard Foster writes "The group fast can be a wonderful and powerful experience provided there is a prepared people who are of one mind in these matters."[30] The person responsible for bringing about this unity of mind and spirit is the man or woman of God led to call the fast. The achievement of oneness in fasting is based on the spiritual leader's ability to clearly articulate the purpose of the fast and the desired outcome to God's people. We have already discussed the nine types of fasts Elmer Towns outlines in his book *Fasting for Spiritual Breakthrough.* While they are not exclusive, they provide a wonderful starting point for identifying a common need among those participating in the corporate fast. I talk more about identifying need in the section on preparation.

Have a clearly defined outcome

Depending on the purpose of the fast, there should be evidence that fasting produces desired results, such as the resolution of conflicts and problems; spiritual maturity; stronger leadership; increased commitment and dedication to the mission of the church, ministry, or group; and an overall heightened sense of awareness and freedom. In other words, it is important to begin with the desired end in mind. Once you are clear about the goal of the fast, you can begin to put in place activities that will lead towards that goal. After the fast has ended, spiritual leaders can determine if the goals of the fast were met by providing surveys to participants. The survey results can prove the power of fasting as well as the effectiveness of the church and its ministries.

Prepare Spiritually and Physically

Because preparing for the fast goes hand-in-hand with establishing the purpose for it, I realize there will be quite a bit of overlap between this section and the one that has just preceded it. Since the purpose for any corporate fast is largely a response to a common need in the spiritual community, it is important that part of the preparation be devoted to identifying what that need is. Often this means naming that which is holding our ministries back, especially if that thing is ourselves. I appreciate Towns's point about leaders taking responsibility and ownership for their shortcomings, as it relates to the Samuel Fast in particular: "The present leadership can't pray, 'They sinned.' That's a cop-out. The current leadership represents the institution where God is not working, and they must pray 'We have sinned.'"[31] The purpose of such an admission is not guilt, but rather the acknowledgement of the work to be done for the body of Christ.

These areas of opportunity can readily be identified because they are often the areas of pain in the church. Pain, whether experienced individually or collectively, slows us down and prevents us from acting. Identifying the areas in which our ministries are lethargic or unproductive can help focus the purpose for the fast. Such periods of examination provide us an opportunity to reflect on the responsibility we have towards those we serve in ministry. In 2 Corinthians 13:5, Apostle Paul admonishes, "Examine yourselves, whether ye be in the faith; prove your own selves. Know ye not your own selves, how that Jesus Christ is in you…" Close examination of ourselves and our ministries enables us to remove obstructions that block our ability to minister effectively. To identify such areas, those in leadership should ask: "Which ministries are demonstrating hurt or lifelessness? What is the source of this pain and how can it best be addressed?"

If the answers to the questions are not obvious, then go directly to the people. Use anonymous surveys to check the pulse of your members to see how they are doing. Ask those in leadership what needs they are currently experiencing in their respective ministries. Then have them to prioritize the list by asking, "Which need, after it has been met, will have the greatest impact on those being served?" Once you have identified a common need and have created a fast around that need, then through prayer and fasting, seek God's guidance about how to fill it.

Further, when calling a fast, it will be important to prepare *all* members. Some will be new to the faith and thus will be unfamiliar with the concept of fasting, so it will be vital for them to understand what fasting is and why fasting is important to a believer's life. Reading and discussing Isaiah 58 collectively is a good place to start. Preparation will also include getting a buy-in. People will be more excited about fasting if they know how it can benefit them on a personal level. Educating groups about the physical, mental, and spiritual benefits discussed earlier may inspire and motivate those who are more reticent to fast.

Indeed, when the purpose of a God-appointed fast is clear, when the vision for the fast has been made plain, everyone in leadership ought to be in on it. Since the goal of the fast is physical, mental, and spiritual preparation to do battle for the Kingdom of God, it is important that the purpose of the fast is highlighted in every ministry. Banners should be flown to signal its coming, announcements should be made well in advance, Sunday School lessons should reiterate its importance, songs chosen for Sunday morning worship service should reverberate its theme, sermons should prepare the people's hearts. Yes, all of these things should work together for those who love God and are called unto His purpose for fasting. The announcement of the corporate fast ought to be an unforgettable moment largely imprinted in the hearts and minds of God's people and equally met with great anticipation and celebration of the great work about to take place.

Allow flexibility in fasting

Although corporate fasts are called to address a common need of the church, how people choose to participate in the fast may be different. Because those who will be fasting will be at different spiritual levels, it is important not to legislate the length of the fast or how people choose to fast. As stated earlier, for fasts where only liquids are consumed, most doctors recommend that first-time fasters do so only for twenty-four hours and then gradually build to longer fasts over a period of time.[32] For longer fasts, you may provide participants the option to fast in round-robin style. This is when individuals, groups, or ministries alternate days and/or times to pray and fast for a specific need.[33] For example, for a twenty-eight day fast that focuses on family, married couples may fast the first week, singles may fast the second week, and children and everyone the last week. Fasting in this way still encourages unity while making the goal of completion attainable for those who are not accustomed to fasting for longer periods.

Spiritual leaders should also recognize that a food fast is not appropriate for everyone, including pregnant women, those who are nursing, youth, those who have a history of eating disorders, or those with prohibitive diets due to health issues.[34] Marjorie Thompson argues the point that Jesus not only fasted from food but also from overusing his power as the

Son of God.[35] Viewed in this light, fasting allows us to refrain from *anything* that prevents us from obeying God's will for us. The fast itself should not become weighed down by rules intended to govern how it should be carried out.

Because corporate fasts are called to address a common area of healing for the church, spiritual leaders will want to remain flexible while encouraging participants to choose a type of fast that addresses the common need. While one person might choose to give up sweets in a fast that focuses on health, another may choose to give up meats. Others may choose a more vegan-style diet that incorporates fruits, vegetables, whole grains, and beans. Still, others may choose to add exercise to their daily regimen. What people choose to release will come from their own recognition of what is blocking them from the collective goal of being a healthier church body. In *Fasting for Your Spiritual Breakthrough,* Towns suggests that fasting participants themselves should determine the purpose, length, and activities they relinquish during their fasts[36] mainly because God is silent on such issues.[37] If God is silent on such issues, then who are we to legislate to others how they ought to conduct their fasts?

Children ought to be considered as well when it comes to fasting. Lynne Baab warns children under twelve should not be involved in fasts that require the abstention of all foods, since it can hinder their growth and development. Instead, she recommends encouraging them to give up a favorite toy, food, or activity.[38] While this is certainly one way of introducing fasting to children, it is equally important that they are able to associate fasting with positive feelings. While some children will eagerly give up a toy that they like, others will resist. Children under the age of twelve may better appreciate fasting if they are able to associate it with gaining, as opposed to losing. Rather than requesting that they give up something, ask them to consider something that they would not ordinarily do like talking to someone at school they never imagined themselves talking to. In this sense, they are gaining a new friend. Or perhaps they can choose to add a vegetable that they would not regularly eat. In this sense, they are potentially adding to the list of foods they like.

Since we are constantly modeling before our children how to live, fasting as a family is perhaps one of the most effective ways of helping children understand the purpose and benefits of fasting. Spiritual leaders can suggest that families fast from TV and allow children to decide how they would like to spend this extra time together. Creating a vision board as a family would help family members bring attention to established values while working towards them. If your church is conducting a Widow's fast, youth ministers can coordinate with soup kitchens or shelters to have youth volunteer for a day. After the experience, the youth can discuss what they gained through helping others. Allowing young people to be involved during the fasting period can teach the values of ministry, family, selflessness, and sharing—all of which are pleasing unto God.

Though corporate fasts bring the body of Christ together for a common spiritual purpose, the way each of us is called to carry out our fast is different. Because each part of the body in Christ is unique, so then is the nature of the fast each of us is called to. Being inclusive and flexible will not only help to unite the body, but it will strengthen it as well. The spiritual leader's role is to call attention to the spiritual moment that has created the opportunity for the fast and invite others to participate. How God leads others to experience the fast is solely up to Him and the individual. Far be it for any of us to legislate another's fast. Since fasting is a time of joy, hope, and renewal, it ought to be an enjoyable experience for everyone.[39]

Celebrate!

Because the end of the fasting period marks the beginning of our journey to receive all that God has revealed to us during the fast, it is worthy of celebration. For some of us, this part of the experience means that we are now physically, mentally, and spiritually prepared to begin the race God has set for us to run. For some of us, it means that we are now unstuck and with clarity of vision, we know where we are headed. For those who may have gotten off track, this part of the journey means our eyes are now focused on the prize of the higher calling. We celebrate because individually we are stronger and by extension, so is the body of Christ. Fasting provides a period of rest and where we had grown tired, we are stronger now with greater resolve to finish what God has begun in us. The purpose of rejuvenation is important because it is during this time that we serve notice to the enemy that we are wiser, stronger, and better than before.

I've already provided ideas for culminating the fast in the previous chapter, but I will mention a couple more here. The testimony is a vital part of the celebration. One way to include this element of celebration is each week to have people deposit in a separate offertory basket at least one benefit they received from fasting. The lists can be compiled and then printed in the bulletin the following weeks as the evidence of the power of fasting. This public testimony may also inspire those who have not fasted to fast and, in a subtle way, may serve as encouragement to others who may be struggling in their fast. A similar idea would be to post large banners in the common area of your church. Invite participants to write the benefits of their fast on the banner. Allow the banner to hang year-round so people are constantly reminded of the power of God to save, heal, and deliver.

Get to Work!

The celebration will be the time to capitalize on everyone's excitement about what God has just done in their lives. They will be hungry now, but in a different way. Because they will have been filled, they will now be eager to go to work for the Kingdom. Have sign-up sheets for people who are interested in ongoing ministries. Equally important, have sign-up sheets for new ministries people are called to. After the celebration, begin to carefully plan how you might minister more effectively. Develop or revisit mission statements, devise action plans, train leaders, and gather the information and resources you need to begin the work of the Higher Calling.

For leaders of the spiritual community, fasting means preparing God's people to do something. It means responding to a common need and having both a vision and a plan for addressing it. This response requires us to "unbusy" ourselves to focus on the work that lies before us. It means demonstrating care for God's people by listening to them, hearing them, and understanding them. We need not look far to find the suffering, the hurt, and the wounded. They sit in our pews every Sunday morning. The question is how are we prepared to help them? The answer is one that has always been available to us, but is rarely used effectively. Choosing to fast with purpose in our churches makes the difference between those who merely go through the motions of ministry and those whose strength of ministry is backed by a people who can earnestly declare that they are better physically, mentally, and spiritually because of it.

Conclusion

Whether you are leading yourself or others, fasting provides the clarity you need to make life better for you and for those with whom you come in contact. By closely examining who you are, fasting empowers you to let go of unhealthy thoughts, feelings, and behaviors so that you can begin to receive those God-like qualities that enable healing, justice, peace, compassion, freedom, contentment, fulfillment, abundance, and love. Ultimately, this is the goal of purposeful fasting. By focusing on the God within you, fasting allows you to control your own destiny and to chart your own success—regardless of what the situation looks like. Fasting helps you to know the voice of God within you so that all that you do is matched with a level of confidence that enables you to lead a meaningful life. What can be more powerful than that?

Imagine what we, our homes, our churches, and communities could look like if we all knew our purpose and freely carried it out. Imagine who we could be if we acted out of the certainty that we were obeying the voice of God within us. Imagine the change that could come about in us and in the world. Imagine the great work that awaits us. Won't you join me?

An Invitation from the Author

Thank you for taking the time to read this book. I hope that it has been a blessing to you. During the time of my writing it, I prayed over my efforts and for everyone this book would reach. So I've been praying for you and for the blessings that God has in store for you. This book is the evidence of my fast, and I'd like to know the impact it has had on others. Won't you write me and let me know how this book has impacted your journey to discovering and carrying out your purpose? You can email me at andrea@highcallcoaching.com or write me at:

High Call Coaching Ministries
P.O. Box 206
Maugansville, MD 21767

May God continue to bless you, and may He that has begun this great work in you perform it until the day of His return!

Appendix of Songs

(Most of these songs are available on YouTube.)

Song	Artist
"I Know Who I Am"	Lakewood
"Nothing Can Separate Me"	Lakewood
"More"	Cece Winans
"I Choose to Worship"	Wess Morgan
"Available"	Melinda Watts
"Yes"	Shekinah Glory
"Prophetic Medley/ The High Place"	LaShun Pace
"Safe"	Phil Wickham

"Resting on His Promise"	Youthful Praise
"The Lifter"	Ted Winn
"He Has His Hands on You"	Marvin Sapp
"My Desire"	Tyrone Powell
"Get Back Up"	TobyMac
"Slow Walk"	Mary Mary
"Move"	Mercyme
"New Season"	Israel and New Breed
"Over"	Youth for Christ
"Freedom"	Eddie James
"Stand Out"	Tye Tribbett & GA
"Get Up"	Mary Mary
"Walking"	Mary Mary
"Light in Me"	Brandon Heath
"Champion"	Darwin Hobbs
"Peace and Favor"	Kurt Carr and the Kurt Carr Singers
"You Hold My World"	Israel Houghton
"Cover the Earth"	Israel Houghton

"Everywhere that I Go"	Israel Houghton
"We Speak to Nations"	Lakewood
"Expect the Great"	Jonathan Nelson
"Faithful to Believe"	Byron Cage
"I Desire More"	Crystal Aikin
"Empty Me"	William Murphy
"Hold On"	TobyMac
"Stay Strong"	Newsboys
"I Shall Live"	Jason Nelson

Endnotes

1. Franklin, Jentezen. *Fasting: Opening the Door to a Deeper, More Intimate, More Powerful Relationship with God.* Lake Mary, FL: Charisma House, 2008.

2. Gregory, Susan. *The Daniel Fast.* Carol Stream, IL: Tyndale, 2010.

3. Franklin, Jentezen. *Fasting Journal: Your Personal 21-day Guide to a Successful Fast.* Lake Mary, FL: Charisma House, 2008.

4. "Religion Among the Millenials." The Pew Forum on Religion and Public Life. The Pew Research Center. http://www.pewforum.org/Age/Religion-Among-the-Millenials.aspx (accessed January 23, 2012).

5. Franklin, Jentezen. *The Fasting Edge: Recover your passion. Recapture your dream. Restore your joy.* Lake

Mary, FL: Charisma House, 2011. Kindle Edition. Location 2012.

6. Foster, Richard J. *Celebration of Discipline: The Path to Spiritual Growth.* 3rd ed. New York: Harpers Collins, 1998. Kindle Edition. 47-48.

7. Weems, Stovall. *Awakening: A New Approach to Faith, Fasting, and Spiritual Freedom.* Colorado Springs: Waterbrook Press, 2010. Kindle Edition. 38.

8. Foster, Richard J. *Celebration of Discipline: The Path to Spiritual Growth.* 49.

9. Towns, Elmer L. *Fasting for Spiritual Breakthrough.* Ventura, CA: Regal, 2001, 2009. Nook Edition.

10. Towns, Elmer. *Fasting for Spiritual Breakthrough.* 15.

11. Centers for Disease Control and Prevention. "Heart Disease." Faststats. http://www.cdc.gov/nchs/fastats/heart.htm (accessed January 23, 2012).

12. Centers for Disease Control and Prevention. "Cancer." Faststats. http://www.cdc.gov/nchs/fastats/cancer.htm (accessed January 23, 2012).

13. Russell, Rex. "Fasting: Giving Our Bodies a Break." 161. Quoted in Towns, Elmer L. *Fasting for Spiritual Breakthrough.* Venura, CA: Regal, 1996.

14. Russell, Rex. "Fasting: Giving Our Bodies a Break." 161.

15. Bragg, Paul C. and Patricia Bragg *The Miracle of Fasting-Proven Throughout History.* Health Science. Kindle Edition. Location 2813.

16. Bragg, Paul C. and Patricia Bragg. *The Miracle of Fasting-Proven Throughout History.* Health Science. Kindle Edition. Location 2884.

17. Bragg, Paul C. and Patricia Bragg. *The Miracle of Fasting-Proven Throughout History.* Health Science. Kindle Edition. Location 4302. Also see Russell, Rex. "Fasting: Giving Our Bodies a Break." 162.

18. Russell, Rex. "Fasting: Giving Our Bodies a Break." 162-64.

19. Baab, Lynne. *Spiritual Freedom Beyond Our Appetites.* Downers Grove, IL: InterVarsity Press, 2006. Kindle Edition. 116.

20. Thompson, Marjorie J. *Soul Feast: An Invitation to the Christian Spiritual Life.* Kindle Edition. Location 1067.

21. Foster, Richard J. *Celebration of Discipline: The Path to Spiritual Growth.* 55.

22. Gregory, Susan. *The Daniel Fast.* 17-18.

23. "Zimbabwe Woman is Oprah's All-Time Best Guest." *The Zimbabwe Mail.* 20 May 2011. (Accessed February 2, 2012).

24. Towns, Elmer. *Fasting for Spiritual Breakthrough* 17 and Bragg, Paul C. and Patricia Bragg. *The Miracle of Fasting-Proven Throughout History.* Health Science. Kindle Edition. Location 1749.

25. Baab, Lynne. *Spiritual Freedom Beyond Our Appetites.* Kindle edition. 117.

26. Baab, Lynne. *Spiritual Freedom Beyond Our Appetites.* Kindle edition. 127.

27. "The Role of the Patriarch in Family Life" in *The* NIV *Archaeological Study Bible,* 30.

28. "The Rights of the Firstborn" in *The* NIV *Archaeological Study Bible, 43.*

29. McKnight, Scot. Fasting. Nashville: Thomas Nelson, 2009. Kindle Edition. 136.

30. Foster, Richard J. *Celebration of Discipline: The Path to Spiritual Growth.* 50.

31. Towns, Elmer L. *Fasting for Spiritual Breakthrough.* 65.

32. Again, I reference Bragg and Bragg and Towns. See note 21.

33. Baab, Lynne. *Spiritual Freedom Beyond Our Appetites*. Kindle edition. 124.

34. Baab, Lynne. *Spiritual Freedom Beyond Our Appetites*. Kindle edition. 28 and 130.

35. Thompson, Marjorie J. *Soul Feast: An Invitation to the Christian Spiritual Life*. Kindle Edition. Location 1105.

36. Towns, Elmer L. *Fasting for Spiritual Breakthrough*. Ventura, CA: Regal, 1996. Nook Edition. 14-15.

37. Towns, Elmer L. *The Beginner's Guide to Fasting*. Ventura, CA: Regal, 2001,2009. Nook Edition. 29.

38. Baab, Lynne. *Spiritual Freedom Beyond Our Appetites*. Kindle edition. 130-31.

39. Weems, Stovall. *Awakening: A New Approach to Faith, Fasting, and Spiritual Freedom*. Kindle Edition. 63.

Bibliography

Baab, Lynne. *Spiritual Freedom Beyond Our Appetites.* Downers Grove, IL: InterVarsity Press, 2006.

Bragg, Paul C. and Patricia Bragg. *The Miracle of Fasting–Proven Throughout History.* Health Science. Kindle Edition.

Centers for Disease Control and Prevention. "Cancer." Faststats. http://www.cdc.gov/nchs/fastats/cancer.htm (accessed January 23, 2012).

Centers for Disease Control and Prevention. "Heart Disease." Faststats. http://www.cdc.gov/nchs/fastats/heart.htm (accessed January 23, 2012).

Foster, Richard J. *Celebration of Discipline: The Path to Spiritual Growth.* 3rd ed. New York: Harpers Collins, 1998. Kindle Edition.

Franklin, Jentezen. *The Fasting Edge: Recover Your Passion. Recapture Your Dream. Restore Your Joy.* Lake Mary, FL: Charisma House, 2011. Kindle Edition.

Franklin, Jentezen. *Fasting: Opening the Door to a Deeper, More Intimate, More Powerful Relationship with God.* Lake Mary, FL: Charisma House, 2008.

Franklin, Jentezen. *Fasting Journal: Your Personal 21-day Guide to a Successful Fast* Lake Mary, FL: Charisma House, 2008.

Gregory, Susan. *The Daniel Fast.* Carol Stream, IL: Tyndale, 2010.

McKnight, Scot. *Fasting.* Thomas Nelson: Nashville, 2009. Kindle Edition.

"Religion Among the Millennials." The Pew Forum on Religion and Public Life. The Pew Research Center. http://www.pewforum.org/Age/Religion-Among-the-Millennials.aspx (accessed January 23, 2012).

"The Rights of the Firstborn" in *The* NIV *Archaeological Study Bible.* 43.

"The Role of the Patriarch in Family Life" in *The* NIV *Archaeological Study Bible*. 30.

Russell, Rex. "Fasting: Giving Our Bodies A Break." 162-164. Quoted in Towns, Elmer L. *Fasting for Spiritual Breakthrough*. Ventura, CA: Regal, 1996. Nook Edition.

Thompson, Marjorie J. *Soul Feast: An Invitation to the Christian Spiritual Life*. Kindle Edition.

Towns, Elmer L. *The Beginner's Guide to Fasting*. Ventura, CA: Regal, 2001, 2009. Nook Edition.

Towns, Elmer L. *Fasting for Spiritual Breakthrough*. Ventura, CA: Regal, 1996. Nook Edition.

Weems, Stovall. *Awakening: A New Approach to Faith, Fasting, and Spiritual Freedom*. Colorado Springs: Waterbrook Press, 2010. Kindle Edition.

"Zimbabwe Woman is Oprah's All-Time Best Guest." *The Zimbabwe Mail*. 20 May 2011. (Accessed February 2, 2012).